Ben's Jigsaw Puzzle

Story by Beverley Randell

Illustrations by Naomi Lewis

Rigby®

A Harcourt Achieve Imprint

www.Rigby.com
1-800-531-5015

"Here you are, Ben," said Mom.

"Here is a jigsaw puzzle."

Ben looked at the box.

"A **dinosaur** puzzle!" he said.

"Thank you, Mom."

4

"I can see the dinosaur's tail," said Ben.

"The tail goes here."

Ben said,

"I am looking for

the dinosaur's legs."

"Here are the legs,"

said Ben.

"The legs go down here."

"You are good at puzzles,"

said Mom.

"Where is the dinosaur's head?"

said Ben.

"Can **you** see

the dinosaur's head, Mom?"

Mom looked and looked.

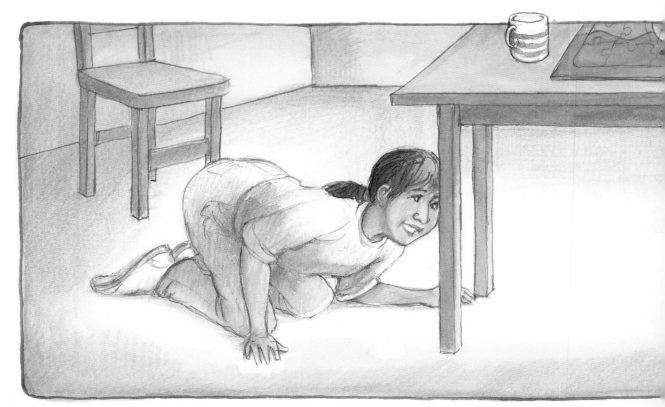

Ben looked and looked.

Ben looked in the box.

"**Here** is the dinosaur's head!"

he said.

"Look at my dinosaur!"

said Ben.